Copyright ©2003 Calvary Press
All rights reserved under International and
Pan-American Copyright Conventions. No part of
this book may be reproduced in any form or by any electronic
or mechanical means including informational storage and retrieval
systems without the expressed permission from the publisher in writing,
except in the case of brief quotations embodied in critical articles or critical reviews.

CALVARY PRESS PUBLISHING
Post Office Box 805
Amityville, NY 11701
1-800-789-8175
www.calvarypress.com

Book design and typography by Advantage Graphics, Inc.
Copiague, New York 631 842-3255

Bianchi, Joseph M.
   My Friend Grace - A Child Learns About The Mercy and
Sovereignty of God / by Joseph M. Bianchi

ISBN 1-879737-52-3
Suggested subject headings:
   1. Christianity – doctrines
   2. Religion
   I. Title

10 9 8 7 6 5 4 3 2 1

My Friend Grace

A Child Learns About The Mercy and Sovereignty of God

Joseph M. Bianchi
Illustrated by Sean Rubin

2003 - Calvary Press, Amityville, New York

It may seem strange to some children, but Annie always looked forward to bedtime. She would get into her most comfortable pajamas, grab her favorite doll, Wendy, snuggle under the covers, and wait for Mom and Dad to make their way into her room.

Annie knew that when her parents arrived, Dad would be carrying a well-worn Bible under his arm, while Mom would still be wearing her apron, having spent the earlier part of the evening preparing dinner and cleaning up. Of course, Annie would help. But now it was time to read God's Word and pray. Annie smiled as she thought of the comfort God's Word brought to her and her family.

As happy as she was, Annie had many questions about the Bible. Mom and Dad had entered the room while she lie in her bed thinking.

"Well, are we ready to read God's Word?" her Mom began.

"Yes, Mom, all ready," Annie said excitedly.

"Ok, then," said Dad, opening that old Bible of his. "Let's continue our reading in the book of Ephesians." Dad adjusted his glasses and then scanned the pages with his finger until he came to the verse where he had left off.

"Ah, here we are, chapter two, verses eight and nine," he said with much satisfaction. "You know Annie, these are some of the most important verses in the Bible. Here, let me read them for you. It says, 'For by grace you have been saved through faith; and that not of yourselves, it is the gift of God; not as a result of works, that no one should boast.'"

Annie's eyes lit up when she heard these verses, but just as quickly, her brow became crinkled, and a frown appeared on her face.

"Dad, at church we always sing songs about grace, but we are also told to love other people and do good works," Annie said. "Now I'm confused. Don't these verses say not to do these things?"

Mom and Dad smiled, proud that their daughter had asked such an important question, and knowing that Annie was eager to learn more about the God who had created all things.

"Annie, listen," Mom said softly. "Did you ever have a good friend who helped you even when you did not deserve it?"

"Oh, yes! Sue is my best friend, she always helps me," Annie exclaimed.

"That's right!" said Mom. "But Annie, imagine you had a friend that could help and save you forever."

"But Mom, now I'm getting more confused."

Dad placed his hand lovingly on Mom's shoulder and said, "Annie, I think Mom is trying to tell you that God's grace is like that friend. You see, grace is receiving a loving act when we really don't deserve it. God's Word says in Romans 5:8 that 'while we were yet sinners, Christ died for us.'"

Mom nodded, and then said, "Yes, you see that's our friend at work, Grace!"

Mom and Dad then began to tell Annie about her new friend, Grace.

Grace, Mom and Dad explained, would save her when she could not save herself. When Annie was in the most dangerous situations of her life, it would be Grace that would save her.

Annie used her imagination to try to understand what Mom and Dad were telling her. She pictured herself on a boat in the midst of a raging sea. She was all alone, and the boat began to sink, the water surrounding her until the waves were crashing over her head. She tried to swim, but it was no use. She called out for help, but her voice was overcome by the sounds of thunder as the storm grew worse.

"Now that would be hopeless," she thought.

Suddenly, a boat appeared with Grace on the deck. She immediately threw a life preserver to Annie, which landed perfectly over her head and then around her waist. She was then pulled safely into the ship and into the arms of Grace. Annie told Mom and Dad about what she had been thinking.

"Yes, Annie, that's a good way of thinking about what grace does," said Dad. "But remember, when Grace threw the life preserver, she didn't ask you if you wanted to be saved or not, did she?"

Annie thought for a moment. "Come to think of it Dad, no she didn't! She just saved me. I was going to die. I was completely helpless!"

Dad smiled his approval. "That's what Jesus did for us, Annie, and that is what grace is all about!"

Mom asked Dad if she could have the Bible for a moment, then turned to Annie and said, "We have been reading through Ephesians in our nightly devotionals with you. Dad a little while ago read Ephesians 2:8 and 9. But let's go back to verse five. It says that 'even when we were dead in our transgressions' that God made us 'alive together' with Christ."

Annie thought again for a moment, and then a look of horror came over her. "Mom," she said gulping hard, "we were…dead?"

"Yes, dear. Oh, not physically dead, but our spirit was dead; we were spiritually dead. We had no power whatsoever in our possession that could save us."

Annie wondered what that would be like. How could somebody be alive on one hand, but dead on the other? She thought that perhaps it would be like being lost in a forest at night. She would certainly be alive, but without a light, she could only feel her way through the woods. She would have to guess if she were going in the right direction. There would be all kinds of scary sounds as wild animals called out to one another. Perhaps she would trip and fall– maybe even hurt herself–but nobody would be there to help her.

"Gee," thought Annie, "I would have no power to help myself. Somebody would have to come and look for me and show me the way out…or I would be lost forever!"

Annie told her parents what she had been thinking. Dad looked over his glasses, his eyes glowing with excitement.

"But, Annie, imagine you were in those woods and suddenly you saw a light in the distance," Dad said. "It got closer and closer, and brighter and brighter. Until suddenly, you realized it was Grace with a lantern. She had found you and was coming to save you. She knew the way out of those dark and dangerous woods. One moment you were lost forever, the next moment you were safely on your way home!"

"Whew!" Annie shouted, "That would be great! That Grace sure is some friend!"

Mother laughed, "She sure is, Annie! I hope you are beginning to understand what God's grace is really all about."

"Yes, Mom, I think I am. If I were in those woods, I would have to rely on somebody else to save me. I could not save myself!"

That's exactly right," Dad said.

"But Dad, what about the good works we do. Doesn't God want us to do good works?"

"Of course he does, Annie." Dad's voice and expression suddenly became very serious. "But nothing that we could do would ever save us."

"Nothing, Dad?"

"No, Annie. Nothing!"

Dad then began to explain again to Annie how mankind had sinned; how the first man and woman, Adam and Eve, had rebelled against God. Now, men and women were lost, just like somebody in a dark forest or a raging sea, with no way to help themselves. Only the grace of God can save them through the Lord Jesus Christ.

"Dad, I still don't quite understand; don't we do something to make Jesus choose us?"

Dad thought for a moment, and then said, "No, Annie, we really don't. Let's imagine that you are outside playing with your friend, Grace. But instead of playing nicely, you act cruelly to her; you call her names, you ignore her when she asks you something, and you laugh at her ideas."

Annie's eyes filled with tears. "Why, that would be horrible. I would never want to do that to my good friend!"

"I know," Dad said, bending over to kiss Annie on the forehead, "but that is exactly what men and women do to the Lord Jesus Christ and God's Word. Now imagine after all the bad things you did to Grace, she did something really nice for you, like giving you a precious gift."

"But Dad," Annie said, "I really wouldn't deserve it!"

"Exactly, Annie! You see no one deserves salvation; it is a gift of God. The Lord Jesus Christ died for sinners despite what they had done, or would do. Matthew 1:21 tells us that Jesus came to save 'His people' from their sins. So you see, even though we don't deserve it, God is merciful and shows us His grace."

Mom stroked Annie's hair. She knew that these were some of the most important questions that Annie would ever ask. "Annie, imagine you were in a giant crowd of people. Everyone is doing something different so there is a lot of confusion. You are in this crowd and you are lost. You ask for help and directions, but nobody seems to care or want to help. Suddenly, you hear Grace's voice calling you. You follow the sound of the voice because you recognize it, and the next thing you know, you are home!"

"Like a sheep, Mom? Isn't that what the Bible says we are…sheep?"

"Yes, Annie. Isaiah 53:6 says, 'All of us like sheep have gone astray,'" Mom said, as she held Annie's hand. Then she opened up Dad's Bible again to John 10: 11. "Listen, Annie, Jesus says that He is the 'good shepherd' who 'lays down his life for the sheep.' The true sheep will only hear His voice, not the voice of others."

"Others?" said Annie as she poked her head up from the pillow. "There are others like Jesus?"

Mom drew her head down close to Annie and looked right in her eyes. "Well, Annie, there are many religions and many people claiming to know the truth, but only our trust in Christ's death on the cross for us can save us. Do you understand?"

"I think I do, Mom. I guess it would be like all of us going on a long trip in a car with my friend, Grace. We get lost and have no idea of how to get where we are supposed to go. Then we come to a whole bunch of road signs all pointing in different directions. We all get confused, but Grace points to one of the signs and says, 'Go that way! That is the only right way to go!'"

Mom reached down and hugged Annie. "Yes, dear, that's the idea. There is only one way to God, and that is through the Lord Jesus Christ. God's grace shows us the right way to go, even though there are many wrong turns we could take."

Annie smiled, but then, once again, a frown appeared on her face. "Mom, I thought God loved everybody. Wouldn't that mean people of other religions, too?"

"Annie, God is merciful even to those who hate Him. After all, don't evil people have homes to live in, families and jobs?"

Dad asked for the Bible and immediately began to turn its pages, then said: "The Bible puts it this way, Annie...let's see, yes, here it is in Matthew 5:45, 'for He causes His sun to rise on the evil and the good, and sends rain on the righteous and the unrighteous.' So God cares for some, but others are the object of His special love."

"You see, Annie," Mom added, "God provides for all, but not all will be saved."

"I guess so, Mom," Annie replied, "but can't people in other religions pray to God and go to heaven, even if they call Him by a different name?"

This was a hard question, and Mom and Dad were quiet for some time before answering.

Finally Dad spoke. "I know that this is something very hard to understand. God's ways, though, are always right; He never makes a mistake! Remember, that Acts 4:12 says, 'there is no other name given among men, by which we must be saved.' Annie, that name is Jesus!"

"Jesus!" Annie exclaimed. Then, Mom and Dad joined in. "Jesus!" they all yelled together.

After much laughter, Mom got serious again. "Annie, imagine you were with a group of friends, Grace being one of them. But instead of calling her Grace, you called her Kathy. Now, let's suppose that Grace had told you many times to call her by her proper name, no nick name or anything like that. Well, do you think that she would like it? Would she listen to what you would have to say?"

"No, Mom, I think she would be upset with me!"

"Well, that is how God feels about His holy name; He wants us to call upon the name of Christ to be saved."

Annie was still a bit concerned. Mom saw the puzzled look on her face. "What's wrong Annie, what's bothering you?"

"Mom, what about all the people in the world that have not heard the name Jesus, how will they get God's grace?"

"Good question!" said Dad. "You see, Christians must tell others that they are separated from God by their sin, and how only Jesus can save them. We do this with unsaved friends, family and even strangers we meet. Missionaries are people who go to foreign lands to spread the good news of the Gospel of Jesus Christ to people who have never heard."

Annie still looked worried. "But will they listen when we tell them? Do people in foreign lands who worship different gods listen to the missionaries?"

"Now Annie," Dad said kindly, "don't you remember your Sunday School lesson on the Great Commission?'

Annie's face lit up with a smile. "Oh, yes! Now I remember. Jesus said in Matthew 28:19 to go into the entire world and preach the Gospel to everyone!"

"Yes, Annie, very good," said Mom. Then once again she opened the old Bible and began flipping pages until she came to that passage. "But the verse before that is perhaps even more important. Jesus tells us there that 'all authority' has been given to Him. So you see Annie, when we preach the Gospel, we rely on God's power, not our own, to change peoples' hearts. And God's grace goes before us."

"There's my friend Grace again," said Annie proudly. "Mom, Dad, God is so good to us, isn't He? He reached down to us when we could not help ourselves, and He provides for all our needs."

Mom and Dad agreed. They were happy that Annie understood how loving God is, and how His ways are always the best ways.

Minutes passed as all three thought about the goodness of God. Finally, Annie broke the silence.

"Mom, Dad, starting today, I'm going to tell everybody I meet about the love of Jesus and how He came to save us…with the help of my friend, Grace!"